W9-ANX-088

BLACK POWER SALUTE

HOW A PHOTOGRAPH CAPTURED A POLITICAL PROTEST

by Danielle Smith-Llera

Content Adviser: Brett Barker, PhD
Associate Professor of History
University of Wisconsin-Marathon County

COMPASS POINT BOOKS
a capstone imprint

Compass Point Books are published by Capstone,
1710 Roe Crest Drive, North Mankato, Minnesota 56003
www.mycapstone.com

Editor: Catherine Neitge
Designers: Tracy Davies McCabe and Catherine Neitge
Media Researcher: Eric Gohl
Library Consultant: Kathleen Baxter
Production Specialist: Laura Manthe

Image Credits
AP Photo: 5, 7, 8, 31, 33, 35, 39, 42, Andrew Harnik, 55, Marco Ugarte, 51; Getty
Images: Bettmann, 19, 47, David Fenton, 21, John Dominis, cover, 11, 29, John
Olson, 9, Keystone-France, 13, Popperfoto, 45, Stringer/Steve Dykes, 49, ullstein
bild, 23; Library of Congress: 15, 18, 22, 56; Lyndon Baines Johnson Library: Robert
Knudsen, 57 (right); Newscom: Dennis Brack, 36, Everett Collection, 25, KRT/Dai
Sugano, 54, 58, KRT/Handout, 57 (left), KRT/Jim Gensheimer, 53, Reuters/Alex
Gallardo, 52, UPI/Jim Ruymen, 59; Photo by Evelyn Floret: 41; Wikimedia: Public
Domain, 17, 27

Library of Congress Cataloging-in-Publication Data
Cataloging-in-publication information is on file with the Library of Congress.
ISBN 978-0-7565-5526-9 (library binding)
ISBN 978-0-7565-5530-6 (paperback)
ISBN 978-0-7565-5542-9 (ebook pdf)

Printed in the United States of America.
10018S17

TABLEOFCONTENTS

ChapterOne
SURPRISE ON THE PODIUM

Tommie Smith stepped into the third lane of the red track for the 200-meter finals in the 1968 Mexico City Olympics. The 24-year-old Californian had already set 11 world track records and was now close to winning a medal for the United States.

Smith believed that his future, and that of other African-Americans, depended on his achieving victory in this race. "It's all or nothing now," he said. He crouched on the track along with sprinters from Europe, the Caribbean, Australia, and the United States, including 23-year-old teammate John Carlos. All eight competitors waited, kneeling with shoes pressed against starting blocks and fingertips balanced at starting lines. "On your marks!" announced an Olympic official. The sprinters raised their hips, muscles tensed. "Get set!"

Smith later remembered only the quiet of the moment. He said he heard "nothing ... but silence."

The starting pistol blasted into the air, and the runners bolted forward. The short race would take them just halfway around the oval track. Carlos took the lead as the group sprinted around the first turn, with Smith lagging a few runners behind him. As the track straightened for the final stretch, Smith caught up with Carlos and, in a final burst of speed,

Tommie Smith jubilantly won the 200-meter sprint in Mexico City, with teammate John Carlos (259) capturing the bronze medal.

moved ahead of his teammate. Ten meters before the finish line, Smith raised his arms victoriously. Smiling, he burst through the tape to win gold with a world record of 19.83 seconds—a record he would hold for 11 years. In another late surge, 26-year-old Peter Norman of Australia had sprinted past Carlos in the last 50 meters of the race to win silver. Carlos won bronze.

Smith and Carlos threw their arms around each other as they walked off the track. They knew something few people watching the race did: a great challenge, perhaps greater than winning the race, lay ahead. "I wasn't there for the race or to win the gold medal as a typical Olympian would be," Carlos said. "I was there to prove something to the world."

Olympic officials uneasily watched the games unfolding. Smith, Carlos, and teammate Lee Evans were members of the Olympic Project for Human Rights, a group of mostly African-American athletes who had nearly refused to participate in the Olympics. OPHR criticized the United States for celebrating their achievements while denying them basic rights. Harry Edwards, an organizer of the group and their professor at San Jose State University in California, said black athletes had "carried the United States on our backs with our victories, and race relations are now worse than ever."

Classmates and teachers of Smith and Carlos at San Jose State gathered around television screens, eagerly waiting for the 200-meter medals ceremony. Professor Steven Millner remembered, "We knew something was going to happen."

For other observers of the Olympics, waiting for the medals ceremony was simply part of their job. Among the photographers with special permission to sit close to the action was John Dominis. He would photograph six Olympics during his two-decade career as a staff photographer for *Life* magazine. He later recalled that he had been "expecting a normal ceremony."

"I wasn't there for the race or to win the gold medal as a typical Olympian would be. I was there to prove something to the world."

Before walking to the track, Smith and Carlos had met in a stadium dressing room to hatch a plan to use their medals ceremony to make a strong statement about racial injustice. "We knew that what we were going to do was far greater than any athletic feat," Carlos said. They had a few props, including a pair of black gloves Smith had brought in case he had to shake hands with Avery Brundage, president of the International Olympic Committee, whom he considered a racist. Norman, the Australian silver medalist, was inspired to join Smith and Carlos, and he suggested that each wear a glove.

The men knew their performance involved great risk. They even feared being shot and killed, just as civil rights leader Martin Luther King Jr. had been a few months earlier.

The trio walked into the brightness of the stadium, following Olympic officials and assistants carrying their medals on velvet pillows. All three athletes wore OPHR badges, but that was just the beginning. Smith and Carlos held shoes behind their backs as they approached the platform. Smith leaned down so an Olympic official could hang the gold medal around his neck. Norman stepped up to receive the silver medal and Carlos the bronze. Noticing that Smith

A black-gloved Smith was congratulated by an Olympic official after receiving his gold medal.

TELLING HISTORY THROUGH PICTURES

Life *magazine's riveting photos brought the Vietnam War home to its millions of readers.*

Life magazine trusted its highly skilled photographers to create images that would bring dramatic stories home to its readers. John Dominis said he appreciated the freedom of having "all the support and money and time, whatever was required, to do almost any kind of work I wanted to do, anywhere in the world."

Henry Luce, the publisher of *Time* magazine, launched the photo-based *Life* magazine in 1936. It featured large photographs spread across glossy pages, accompanied by short captions. Sales of the magazine soon topped 1 million a week.

In the 1960s, gripping photographs on *Life's* cover and inside pages showed politicians, celebrities, and the space program. The covers sometimes presented highly emotional images, such as the limp body of a boy injured during civil rights riots and the face of Martin Luther King Jr.'s widow under a black veil of mourning. Through the magazine, readers saw photographs of the violence and death of the Vietnam War.

As increasing numbers of readers turned to television for their stories and pictures, *Life* magazine became less popular. In 1972 the magazine stopped publishing weekly editions, and starting in 2004, it appeared as a newspaper supplement for a few years. It ceased publication in 2007.

and Carlos were each wearing single black gloves, the official thought they had hurt their hands.

Following tradition, the three men turned to face the U.S. flag as it rose up the flagpole. To honor the U.S. gold medal winner, "The Star Spangled Banner" was played, and Smith and Carlos bowed their heads. At this point the traditional medals ceremony took an unforgettable turn—Smith and Carolos each raised a black-gloved fist into the air. For the 90-second anthem, athletes, Olympic officials, and spectators all stood at attention for what one observer said felt like an "absolute eternity."

Just 20 feet (6 meters) away, Dominis captured a tight shot of the three medalists framed by dark sky. Then it was over. But photos made by Dominis and others ensured that the world saw what they did. The image reached the millions of people who read the November 1 issue of the popular weekly newsmagazine *Life*. The accompanying article was headlined "A Stubborn Protest Jars the Games: Amid Gold Medals, Raised Black Fists." Dominis' photograph also ensured that the silent demonstration would be remembered, and eventually admired, as a symbol of the struggle for civil rights and, in the words of John Carlos, of an "equal chance to be a human being."

For the 90-second anthem, athletes, Olympic officials, and spectators all stood at attention for what one observer said felt like an "absolute eternity."

The 1968 silent protest by Olympic champions still resonates today.

ChapterTwo
DEMANDING RIGHTS

Tommie Smith and John Carlos were not the only ones to use the 1968 Olympic Games to draw attention to injustice. Just 10 days before the opening ceremonies, thousands of students gathered in a plaza in the Tlatelolco neighborhood of Mexico City to protest police brutality and the government's takeover of their universities. They chanted, "We don't want Olympic Games! We want revolution!"

The consequences of the peaceful protest were grisly. Bullets bounced off the buildings as police and soldiers shot at the unarmed students, killing an unknown number, but likely hundreds. Still, Avery Brundage of the IOC and Mexican officials decided to continue with the games. Protesters splattered the white doves of peace on Olympic banners with blood-red paint as a reminder of the massacre.

Peace gave way to unrest and violence that year in many parts of the world. In American, European, and Asian cities, young people marched in the streets, challenging the authority of university administrations and governments that they felt were too controlling. They hoisted banners and sometimes tossed bricks and homemade explosives when police and soldiers met them with bullets and sometimes tanks.

Peaceful protests against the Vietnam War were widespread in the United States during the late 1960s.

Many protesters were calling for an end to the Vietnam War. In the United States, many were also calling for the end of conflict at home. African-American students and their white supporters protested peacefully against discrimination. The injustice and brutality faced by African-Americans in the late 1960s had deep roots. More than two centuries of brutal abuse of enslaved Africans and their descendants was supposed to have ended after the Civil War. In theory, the 14th Amendment to the U.S. Constitution in 1868 granted citizenship and equal rights to all, including people newly freed from slavery. Yet for the next century the 14th Amendment was ignored, and African-Americans, even though they were U.S. citizens, could not exercise even the basic rights they were guaranteed by the Constitution.

For decades the federal government acted as if black citizens had the same opportunities white citizens did. But while the 15th Amendment, in 1870, granted African-American men the right to vote, they struggled for decades to exercise it. State governments in the South made rules to prevent black voters from casting ballots. Potential voters were discouraged by literacy tests, poll taxes, and unnecessarily complicated registration procedures. In 1940, just 3 percent of eligible African-American voters in southern states were registered to vote.

Many African-Americans also had little freedom to choose jobs—even after the end of slavery. For decades after the Civil War, many continued working for former masters as servants. Others worked in the fields of former slave owners. White landowners avoided paying them wages by allowing their families to grow crops on their land. In return, they owed the landowner a share of their harvest—even if crops failed. Debt quickly mounted for these sharecropper families. Some southern blacks moved north and later west, but they often found the same problems they

The lives of sharecroppers in the South were not easy after the Civil War.

were trying to escape. Even in the 1950s and 1960s, job opportunities for blacks were so limited—even in fast-growing California—that from an early age Tommie Smith and Lee Evans helped support their families by working as sharecroppers picking cotton and grapes. Evans recalls working on his feet for 12 hours a day.

Black citizens faced inequality in the workplace—and everywhere else. They were forced to live apart from whites and to send their children to separate, inferior schools. In the South, they were not allowed in certain stores or restaurants and had to sit at the backs of buses. The U.S. Supreme Court ruled that this segregation was legal as long as facilities were "separate but equal," although in reality they were never equal.

In 1954 the Supreme Court ruled that segregation in schools was unconstitutional, and U.S. laws finally began to protect the rights of black citizens. But the process of desegregation was slow. Many whites resisted the changes. As African-Americans struggled for equality, they continued to endure harassment, physical violence, and even murder.

Smith and Carlos were not the first to openly— and peacefully—protest unjust treatment of African-Americans. In 1955 activists took the battle for equality to city streets. Rosa Parks was arrested and fined for refusing to give up her bus seat to a white passenger in Montgomery, Alabama. On the day of her court hearing, the city's black residents began a bus boycott that lasted more than a year. Like Parks, the Reverend Dr. Martin Luther King Jr., a boycott leader, believed in peaceful protest and what he called citizens' "moral responsibility to disobey unjust laws."

The peaceful protest in Montgomery caught the nation's attention. The U.S. Supreme Court ordered the city to desegregate its buses. Yet the battle for the right to sit anywhere on southern buses continued. Black passengers were often attacked by mobs, and sometimes the passengers were arrested and jailed.

As African-Americans struggled for equality, they continued to endure harassment, physical violence, and even murder.

Rosa Parks' arrest in Montgomery, Alabama, sparked a successful bus boycott that would change the lives of African-Americans.

Even when faced with injury or death, King and other activists continued to organize and inspire peaceful protests. On February 1, 1960, four African-American students ordered coffee at a whites-only lunch counter in Greensboro, North Carolina. The nonviolent protest inspired others to do the same at other whites-only restaurants. Protesters

Martin Luther King Jr. spoke to hundreds of thousands of demonstrators at the Lincoln Memorial in 1963.

did not fight back, even when attacked by racial slurs, pelted with food, or kicked. If arrested, other volunteers took their places at the counters.

On August 28, 1963, King once again proved to the world the power of the peaceful demonstration. This time he gathered 200,000 people, both black and white, in the nation's capital in support of a civil

Alabama state troopers brutally attacked civil rights protester John Lewis during an attempted peaceful march in 1965. The civil rights leader was elected to Congress in 1986 and has represented Georgia's 5th District ever since.

rights bill proposed by President John F. Kennedy. Outside the Lincoln Memorial, King declared to the crowd, "I have a dream that my four little children will one day live in a nation where they will not be judged by the color of their skin but by the content of their character." In July 1964, the Civil Rights Act became law, forbidding discrimination in employment based on gender or race and segregation in public schools and other institutions.

But the new legislation still failed to protect African-Americans from injustice in their daily lives. On March 7, 1965, the nation's TV sets showed images of bloodied protesters being beaten by Alabama police and state troopers. Nonviolent demonstrators had been trying to march from Selma to Montgomery, Alabama's capital city, in support of voting rights. Many Americans were outraged by "Bloody Sunday." The sacrifices of the protesters helped pass the federal Voting Rights Act of 1965 five months later. By the end of the year, 250,000 new black voters had been registered in the United States.

The new laws did not end the frustration in poor African-American communities. Black residents in the Watts neighborhood of Los Angeles had long faced unemployment and poor schools and housing. When police scuffled with an unarmed young black man after stopping his car in August 1965, riots raged for six days, leaving 34 people dead and more than 1,000 wounded.

Some young African-Americans grew tired of King's nonviolent approach. They were angry at those who abused peaceful protesters. Activist Stokely Carmichael described seeing "those young kids on TV, getting back up on the lunch counter stools after being knocked off them, sugar in their eyes, ketchup in their hair—well, something happened to me. Suddenly I was burning."

Many frustrated young African-Americans turned to a leader with a much different approach to the struggle against discrimination than King. A young black leader named Malcolm X declared that nonviolent protest left blacks "defenseless."

By the end of the year, 250,000 new black voters had been registered in the United States.

Stokely Carmichael was an early leader of the Student Nonviolent Coordinating Committee. He would spend his life fighting for civil rights.

As the charismatic spokesperson of a religious group called the Nation of Islam, he advised followers to "be peaceful, be courteous, obey the law, respect everyone; but if someone puts his hand on you, send him to the cemetery."

King dreamed of a future when blacks and whites "will be able to join hands … as sisters and brothers." But Malcolm X urged African-Americans to reject white society and live separately. Nation of Islam members, commonly called Black Muslims, chose new names to replace the family names assigned to their ancestors by slave owners. The men often wore North African style caps. The group published a newspaper, built temples, and set up its own schools, stores, and restaurants.

The Autobiography of Malcolm X, by Alex Haley, published shortly after the assassination, would become a classic.

On February 21, 1965, Nation of Islam rivals assassinated 39-year-old Malcolm X, leaving many young African-Americans shocked at the loss of a leader. But they remembered his advice to fight for justice, freedom, and equality not by peaceful protest but "by any means necessary." This new attitude among black activists in the mid-1960s even popularized a new term. In 1966 Stokely Carmichael

AN ATHLETE TAKES A STAND

Muhammad Ali (right) would eventually win his court battle and return to the boxing ring.

John Dominis willingly went to Vietnam, armed with his cameras, to document the lives of people caught up in the Vietnam War.

But many young American men went unwillingly, because they were drafted and forced to serve in the military. A disproportionate number of the draftees were African-Americans. From late 1966 to mid-1969, 41 percent of the soldiers chosen to fight in the war were African-Americans. At the time, blacks made up only 11 percent of the U.S. population.

The Black Panther Party issued a protest. It said that "black people should not be forced to fight in the military service to defend a racist government that does not protect us. We will not fight and kill other people of color in the world who, like black people, are being victimized by the white racist government of America. We will protect ourselves from the forces and violence of the racist police and the racist military, by whatever means necessary."

A famous African-American boxing champion, Muhammad Ali, was a Nation of Islam member, and he shared this view. In 1967 he refused to be drafted. "It is in the light of my consciousness as a Muslim minister and my own personal convictions," he said, "that I take my stand in rejecting the call to be inducted in the armed services. I do so with the full realization of its implications and possible consequences." The consequences included a fine and a prison sentence. "I have searched my conscience," he said, "and I find I cannot be true to my belief in my religion by accepting such a call." As a result, Ali was stripped of his world heavyweight title and not allowed to box professionally. He went almost four years without fighting. But he protested in the courts, and he won his legal battle in 1971. The U.S. Supreme Court ruled that the government should not have tried to force Ali into the military, given his religious beliefs against war.

told an audience in Mississippi about a new way of protesting. For years, he said, activists had been chanting "Freedom!" while facing police officers with powerful water hoses and dogs. "What we are going to start saying now," Carmichael said, "is 'Black Power!'" The crowd shouted the phrase back and soon it was being heard at demonstrations across the country.

The term "black power" sounded aggressive, and its use alarmed many people. King called the new phrase "an unfortunate choice of words." But many young African-Americans, like college students Huey Newton and Bobby Seale, embraced it. In 1966 they founded the Black Panther Party for Self-Defense in Oakland, California, a city simmering with tension between police and the black community. Many white leaders were frightened by the appearance of these new kind of activists, who wore black, military-style berets and black jackets and saluted with raised fists. Their openly displayed guns stirred fears of violence.

Black Panther members were part of a new wave of activists who took a fierce pride in being not just Americans, but African-Americans. They studied African history. They allowed their naturally curly hair to grow and wore beads and colorful, boldly printed clothing like that of their ancestors. They organized community programs that offered free breakfasts, and they ran clothing drives. They offered job training, health clinics, and legal aid to the poor.

Black Panther Party members marched in protest in 1968.

But as the Black Panther Party and other groups inspired by the idea of "black power" began appearing in many U.S. cities, government authorities grew uneasy. Events in the summer of 1967 convinced many of them that the black power movement was dangerous. In July, a peaceful protest in Newark, New Jersey, over the brutal treatment of a black taxicab driver by police turned violent. Rioters threw explosives, smashed windows, and looted shops.

In Detroit, Michigan, the arrest of black partygoers at an unlicensed bar sparked riots and fires that spread across the city. It took thousands of National Guardsmen to stop the unrest, which left 43 people dead, hundreds wounded, and thousands arrested. A government commission that studied the reasons for the riots said in 1968 that the United States was "moving toward two societies, one black, one white—separate and unequal."

The violent death of an important black leader on April 4, 1968, stunned the nation. While in Memphis, Tennessee, to support a strike by garbage collectors, Martin Luther King Jr. was shot and killed at his hotel. President Lyndon B. Johnson urged Americans to remember that "only by joining together ... [can we] continue to move toward equality." A week later Congress passed the Fair Housing Act, advancing the civil rights mission another step. The law made it illegal to deny anyone housing based on race, gender, nationality, or religion.

Sadness following the loss of King became anger across the nation. News of the assassination triggered riots. Mobs looted stores and set fires in Boston, Chicago, Washington, D.C., and more than 100 other U.S. cities. Government officials accused black power organizations of further stirring up unrest. Black Panther Party members faced off with police in deadly gun battles. The director of the Federal Bureau of Investigation (FBI) announced in

The United States was "moving toward two societies, one black, one white— separate and unequal."

The 1964 meeting between King (left) and Malcolm X lasted one minute. Both men were assassinated at age 39, before they could work together for civil rights.

1969 that "the Black Panther Party, without question, represents the greatest threat to the internal security of the country." The organization began to break up as its leaders were jailed and as disagreements divided the group.

Even though King and Malcolm X disapproved of each other's methods, and only briefly met in person once by accident, they both influenced young African-Americans like Smith and Carlos in the 1960s. "Dr. King wants the same thing I want," said Malcom X. "Freedom!"

ChapterThree
PORTRAIT OF A PROTEST

In a year of smashed windows and homemade explosions, Tommie Smith and John Carlos' silent protest at the 1968 Olympic Games "actually passed without much general notice in the packed Olympic Stadium," according to *The New York Times*. Even photographer John Dominis said he "hardly noticed what was happening when I was shooting." He said the quiet scene on the medals platform did not seem like "a big news event."

But Dominis captured the event on 35mm black and white film. By doing that, he helped make the silent protest news, and eventually history. At a press conference shortly after the event, Smith said, "Black America will understand what we did tonight." It was explained that Smith "had raised his right fist to represent black power in America, while Carlos raised his left fist to represent black unity. Together they formed an arch of unity and power."

Dominis' photograph captured many details that spectators could have easily missed. Smith and Carlos stood shoeless, in black socks. Smith wore a black scarf, and Carlos wore a string of beads. Smith said the scarf "represented black pride and the black socks with no shoes stood for black poverty in racist America." Carlos said he wore the beaded necklace

Smith and Carlos said their raised fists formed an arch of unity and power.

"to represent the thousands of anonymous black Americans who were lynched at the hands of white racists." His jacket was unzipped, he said, because "I was representing shift workers, blue-collar people, and the underdogs. That's why my shirt was open. Those are the people whose contributions to society are so important but don't get recognized."

After the press conference, Smith refused to speak publicly about the event for more than 20 years, but Carlos did. Years later Carlos told an interviewer that there was never fear or doubt about their protest. "It was a matter of us getting out there, and setting the world on fire, resurrecting people's consciousness, making people wonder what could be so wrong to make those guys do something like that," he said.

There was no need to look beyond their college campus to find an example of the discrimination that made young African-Americans of the 1960s so determined, and so impatient, for change. In beautiful northern California, San Jose State looked like a place of enormous opportunity for young African-Americans. Scholarships made going to college possible for promising black athletes like Smith and his Olympic teammate Lee Evans. Both of them had grown up picking crops to help support their families. Carlos grew up in the poor New York City neighborhood of Harlem and listened to speeches by Malcolm X.

Track was an obvious choice for athletes who could not afford expensive equipment or club memberships. Without easy access to pools, Carlos, for example, had given up his dream of becoming a competitive swimmer. Australian Peter Norman, who was raised in a working-class family, chose track after being lent a second-hand pair of running shoes.

Tommie Smith broke the
tape in the 400 meters to
set a world record in 1967.
San Jose State teammate Lee
Evans was not far behind.

Smith, Carlos, and Evans joined the famous track
team that earned San Jose the nickname "Speed
City." Celebrated coach Bud Winter recruited young
men and groomed them to become champions. In his
35-year career, Winter coached 27 Olympians.

But even though white and black students were
part of the same sports teams at San Jose State, life
off the athletic fields was very much different. The
university's student government was mostly white.
Social clubs called fraternities did not accept black
members. White landlords often refused to rent
off-campus apartments to black students.

Many black students at San Jose State found the injustice intolerable. "We were ... a generation of movers," Smith recalled. "Nothing was going to change unless someone made a step to do so." He, Carlos, and Evans were not Black Panthers, but new ideas of "black power" inspired them. Track champion Rafer Johnson, who won Olympic gold eight years before the Mexico City Games, wrote in his autobiography about the black power movement. "The militant tactics of Stokely Carmichael, H. Rap Brown, Angela Davis, and Malcolm X seemed divisive and destructive. Still, I was glad they were around. They dared to utter truths that others could not, and their fervor accelerated the process of social change. The larger society might have never awakened if those fierce, threatening voices had not been raised."

San Jose State's athletics department simmered with the frustration of the black athletes. "It is very discouraging," Smith told reporters in 1967, "to be in a team with white athletes. On the track you are Tommie Smith, the fastest man in the world, but once you are in the dressing rooms you are nothing more than a dirty Negro."

Black athletes also felt neglected in the classroom. A sociology professor on the campus, Harry Edwards, had attended San Jose State on an athletic scholarship and knew this experience first-hand. Coach Winter recruited Smith, but it was

"The larger society might have never awakened if those fierce, threatening voices had not been raised."

Edwards who told him, "You're coming here to get an education, not to run fast."

Wearing a black beret, beads, and sunglasses, Edwards brought the bold attitude of the black power movement to the students in his courses. In 1968 Smith said, "I took a class in black leadership. It started me thinking: What the hell is going on in the U.S.? I'm a human. What kind of rights do I have? What kind of rights don't I have? Why can't I get these rights?"

Edwards encouraged his students to go outside the classroom and take bold action. When it came to standing up for basic rights, he said, "The Black Panther Party set a new bar in terms of what was accessible. Those suit-wearing days were over with. You didn't have to be polite. In … fact, the thing now was to get in their face." He organized campus protests against racial discrimination that drew both black and white students and faculty members. He and his supporters gave university officials a list of demands in 1967. Among them were hiring more black professors and coaches and adding housing for black students. When no changes came, Edwards and others organized a protest that caused the first football game of the season to be canceled.

That fall Edwards saw the greatest opportunity of all for calling attention to the racism faced by black athletes and others. The approaching 1968 Olympics would gather teams from around the world to compete for medals and glory for their countries. Edwards helped activist students like Evans, Smith, Carlos, and others form the Olympic Project for Human Rights. The group wanted black athletes to boycott the 1968 games to protest racism. In addition, they demanded the ouster of IOC President Avery Brundage, the hiring of more black coaches, and the expulsion of segregated South Africa.

In a 1967 interview, Smith asked, "Why should we participate for a country and are [still] denied some of the rights that should be given us legally from 1865?" Of the proposed boycott, Brundage said, "If these boys are serious, they're making a very bad mistake."

A protester hoisted a sign during the 1968 Olympic Trials in Los Angeles.

Others also disapproved of the threatened boycott. OPHR members received hate mail threatening them with violence, even death. Edwards' pet dogs were killed, and he was followed by the FBI.

Brundage scolded OPHR for tainting the games with disagreements. "In Olympic circles," he said, "the word boycott is not used. That's a political word." Yet famed baseball player Jackie Robinson, the first African-American to play in the major leagues, admired the activists. "I respect their courage," he said. "We need to understand the reason and frustration behind these protests … it was different in my day, perhaps we lacked courage."

Martin Luther King Jr. also approved of OPHR's proposed boycott. In 1968 in New York, he met with Edwards, Smith, Carlos, and other black athletes who were willing to give up years of intense training by staying home instead of competing in the Olympics. He said, "No one looking at these … demands can ignore the truth of them. … Freedom always demands sacrifice and … they have the courage to say 'We're going to be men and the United States of America have deprived us of our manhood, of our dignity and our native worth, and consequently we're going to stand up and make the sacrifices.'" King even offered

Martin Luther King Jr. would be assassinated before he could do more work with the Olympic protesters.

to organize a protest in Mexico City. But he was assassinated six months before the Olympics.

Grief and outrage caused by King's death drove more athletes to consider the boycott. African-American long-jumper Ralph Boston said, "I sat and thought about it and I see that if I go to Mexico City and represent the United States I would be representing people like the one that killed Dr. King. And there are more people like that. On the other hand, I feel if I don't go and someone else wins the medal and it goes to another country, I haven't accomplished anything either."

OPHR also won the support of a group of white athletes who sympathized with their concerns. Members of the U.S. Olympic crew team, who were all rowers from Harvard University, made a public statement: "We—as individuals—have been concerned about the place of the black man in American society in their struggle for equal rights. As members of the U.S. Olympic team, each of us has come to feel a moral commitment to support our black teammates in their efforts to dramatize the injustices and inequities which permeate our society."

The IOC finally gave in to just one demand and barred South Africa from the games. But support among OPHR athletes for a boycott was crumbling. They had worked too hard to give up a chance to compete in the most prestigious sports event in the world.

Edwards finally gave up on a boycott, but he urged the athletes to find their own way to protest. He told them that "everybody is free to do what they feel their commitment permits them to do." When the games opened, Olympic officials were worried about what might happen. Smith had warned the public to "expect almost anything."

Anxious IOC officials sent Olympic legend Jesse Owens to persuade the OPHR athletes not to disrupt the games. The African-American track champion had won four gold medals at the 1936 Olympics in Berlin, a spectacular achievement showing that Adolf Hitler's claims of white Germans' "superiority" were a racist lie. Now 55 years old, Owens echoed Brundage when he said that "there is no place in the athletic world for politics."

But the African-American athletes were not impressed. When Owens told them they would never get jobs if they protested, Evans responded, "We can't find a job now." The athletes were saddened by how life had turned out for the Olympic champion who struggled to find work after the Berlin Games. But they were upset that Brundage sent Owens to talk to them. "Jesse was confused as far as I'm concerned," said Evans. "So he came and talked to us ... really talking stupid to us and we just shouted him out of the room. I still admire him to this day, that's why I say he was confused coming to talk to us like that because we knew that he was being victimized. He was a victim and we felt sorry for him actually."

THE THIRD MAN

Peter Norman (111) tied an Olympic record on his way to the medal round at the 1968 Olympics.

Silver medalist Peter Norman's life changed forever when he told Smith and Carlos, "I will stand with you," and stepped onto the victory stand at the Mexico City Olympics. At that time, his native Australia had racial troubles of its own, including tight restrictions on non-white immigration into the country. Norman's role in the 1968 protest earned him deep scorn. "As soon as he got home he was hated," said his nephew Matthew Norman, who made a film called *Salute!* about his uncle.

Norman's silver-medal winning 200-meter dash set an Australian record, yet he was not invited to compete in the 1972 Munich Olympics, and Australia entered no one in the sprint events. "I would have dearly loved to go to Munich [but] I'd earned the frowning eyes of the powers that be in track and field," he said in the film *Salute!* "I'd qualified for the 200 meters 13 times and

100 meters five times [but] they'd rather leave me home than have me [in Munich]."

Norman said he had no regrets about what he did. "I have to confess, I was rather proud to be part of it." Norman died of a heart attack in 2006. Tommie Smith and John Carlos traveled to his funeral in Australia to serve as pallbearers. "He didn't raise his fist," Smith said about their 1968 protest, "but he did lend a hand."

Norman's place in history did not receive widespread recognition until after his death. "It's just one of those tales that I think ought to be better known," said Andrew Leigh, a member of Australia's Parliament. "I, as an Aussie, should have been brought up on Peter Norman, but I wasn't." He pointed out that Norman was "on the right side of history when so many others were on the wrong side."

As the 200-meter medal winners walked to the stadium, photographer John Dominis waited. A former assistant managing editor at *Life* has praised Dominis as one of the most modest "great photographers" he knew. "He had his finger on the trigger all the time," Richard B. Stolley said, and he had "a remarkable calmness." Dominis enjoyed working sports sidelines, having attended college on a football scholarship. But in his career he had also photographed soldiers scrambling for cover in Korea and doing drills in Vietnam. His camera captured wild African cats and the private moments of camera-shy celebrities.

Dominis usually carried Nikon F 35mm cameras with long lenses and hung a Leica 35mm camera on a strap around his neck. Using the lightweight German Leica, he once snapped a humpback whale in midair above the sea near Bermuda. After waiting weeks for the right moment, he got the image of the whale with one shot.

The right moment for the Olympic athletes to make their statement came as the national anthem began. "There's something awful about hearing 50,000 people go silent, like being in the eye of a hurricane," Carlos said. Dominis used 35mm film to shoot a tight image of the athletes with their arms raised. Other photographers took wider images that included Olympic officials standing awkwardly

John Dominis, who died in 2013 at age 92, served in the army as a combat photographer during World War II. He spent more than 20 years at *Life* magazine.

around the victory stand. Years later, Carlos admitted, "I had no idea the moment on the medal stand would be frozen for all time. I had no idea what we'd face."

Brundage and others wasted no time publicly scolding the athletes. U.S. Olympic Committee (USOC) officials said their demonstration was "immature behavior" that went against "the basic standards of sportsmanship and good manners." They took swift action. Smith and Carlos were sent home and banned from ever competing in the Olympics again.

The actions of the Olympic officials turned the quiet protest into headline news. "There was nothing but a raised fist in the air and a bowed head, acknowledging the American flag—not symbolizing a hatred for it," Smith explained. Former USOC publicist Robert Paul admitted decades later that if the organization "had handled the whole affair right, with some reason, tolerance and common sense, it would have been something we could now look back on with pride. Instead, it's the Olympics' biggest ongoing shame."

"Their powerful silent protest in the 1968 Games was controversial, but it woke folks up and created greater opportunity for those that followed."

The U.S. Olympic Committee took a step toward erasing that shame in 2016 when it asked Smith and Carlos to serve as Olympic ambassadors. The pair joined 2016 Team USA members for a ceremony at the White House. "Their powerful silent protest in the 1968 Games was controversial, but it woke folks up and created greater opportunity for those that followed," said President Barack Obama.

But in the eyes of many in 1968, the minute and a half on the victory stand turned three heroes into three traitors. It made little difference that Smith was the only man in the history of track and field to hold 11 world records simultaneously or that Carlos returned to the United States to help San Jose State win its first national championship in 1969. Finding work was difficult for them. Carlos later remembered burning furniture to keep his family warm. Strangers spat on them in the street. The received hundreds of death threats in the mail.

Carlos said living with the hostility "was almost like we were on a deserted island. ... But we survived." Eventually they returned to school campuses to work with young people. Smith spent three decades as a college professor and coach. Carlos coached and worked as a high school counselor. He hopes to inspire young people to action, telling them, "You have the same courage I had. You just need to know who you are."

Chapter Four

FROM TRAITORS TO HEROES

When Tommie Smith and John Carlos raised their fists on the victory stand, they knew that Martin Luther King Jr. would have approved. Carlos recalls King's telling him and other athletes in the Olympic Project for Human Rights that an Olympic protest would affect the world the way, when a rock drops, "ripples go out to the far end of the lake." In this way, John Dominis' photograph helped carry the image far beyond Mexico City's stadium, first through magazines and much later in history books. Brundage himself "multiplied the impact of the protest a hundredfold" by "throwing a fit" and punishing the athletes, sportswriter Red Smith pointed out.

The next day another pair of African-American track team members made a silent statement on the victory stand. Dominis had captured a heart-warming photo of Bob Beamon being helped by teammates after collapsing upon learning he'd set a world record in the long jump—one that would stand for nearly 23 years. Teammate Ralph Boston, who won the bronze medal, remembered feeling they had to "make some sort of statement." Despite the dismissal of Smith and Carlos from their team, or perhaps because of it, Boston stepped onto the victory

With pants rolled up to show his black socks, Bob Beamon received the gold medal for his record-shattering long jump.

stand barefooted and with what he called a "defiant look." Beamon accepted his gold medal with his pants rolled up to reveal black socks.

San Jose State viewers "couldn't wait" for Lee Evans' event, said former professor Steven Millner. After all, Evans was the influential OPHR cofounder who had first encouraged Smith to attend an OPHR meeting. When his teammates were dismissed, Evans was so upset that he wanted to leave Mexico City. But he said later that Smith and Carlos "came to me and said I better run and I better win." Evans not only won the 400-meter race with a world record that he held for 20 years, but he also saw his chance to send another message to the world.

As Evans and his medal-winning African-American teammates approached the victory stand, San Jose State supporters were thrilled to see the athletes wore berets. Evans later explained, "We knew that the black beret was a symbol of the Black Panther Party. … I thought they were pretty brave guys, but I wouldn't do what they were doing. … So my job [protesting at the Olympics] was easy. This is one of the things I learned from Malcolm X and Martin Luther King. Everybody can play a part but everyone has to do something."

But some supporters were disappointed with the medal winners' performance. During the national anthem, the medalists removed their berets respectfully. Instead of wearing a solemn expression like Smith, Carlos, Beamon, and Boston, Evans smiled and waved at the audience. He later admitted he had been "scared to death" and "figured it would be hard to shoot a guy with a big smile." Years later, Millner said

"This is one of the things I learned from Malcolm X and Martin Luther King. Everybody can play a part but everyone has to do something."

he understood Evans' difficult position. He asked, "What could you do beyond what Tommie and John had done?"

Evans found himself in a frustrating position. "I had a tough time, too because the blacks thought that I didn't do enough and the whites were just mad. I got it from both sides," he later said. He spent years coaching outside the United States. "I decided to work in Africa, to help Africans," he said. "This is my contribution. The movement became my career."

The effects of Smith and Carlos' protest and dismissal continued to ripple through the Olympic Village in Mexico City. The U.S. women's 400-meter relay team dedicated their gold medal to them. Mark Spitz, a gold medalist on the U.S. swim team, said the protest "resonated with me because I had felt the sting of anti-Semitism, and they certainly shouldn't have been kicked out of the Olympic Village for a silent protest that hurt no one."

But outside the Olympic Village, many saw Smith and Carlos' actions as hurtful. The *Chicago Tribune* called the act "an embarrassment visited upon the country" and "an insult to their countrymen." The *Los Angeles Times* described the raised arms and fists as a "Nazi-like salute." Even though the track team won 15 gold medals, the U.S. government kept the athletes at a distance. Smith and Carlos' teammate Mel Pender later said, "There has never been an Olympic team like ours and yet we are the only one that didn't go to the White House. That still sticks with me. The salute holds a lot of significance to the guys that

TRADITION OF PROTEST

With their actions at the 1968 Olympics, Tommie Smith, John Carlos, and Peter Norman showed that athletes could grab the world's attention with silent protests. Athletes today continue to publicly point out injustices.

National Basketball Association stars Carmelo Anthony, Chris Paul, LeBron James, and Dwyane Wade opened the 2016 ESPY awards ceremony in Los Angeles with a call for social change. Just a week before the July ceremony, two more African-American men had been killed in police shootings—this time in Louisiana and Minnesota. After the shootings, five police officers had been murdered at a peaceful demonstration in Dallas, Texas.

"Generations ago, legends like Jesse Owens, Jackie Robinson, Muhammad Ali, John Carlos and Tommie Smith, Kareem Abdul-Jabbar, Jim Brown, Billie Jean King, Arthur Ashe and countless others, they set a model for what athletes should stand for," said Chris Paul of the Los Angeles Clippers. "So we choose to follow in their footsteps."

Superstar LeBron James urged "all professional athletes to educate ourselves, explore these issues, speak up, use our influence and renounce all violence and, most importantly, go back to our communities, invest our time, our resources, help rebuild them, help strengthen them, help change them. We all have to do better."

At the same time Women's National Basketball Association players and team owners made their own political statements. Members of several teams wore black warm-up shirts or black T-shirts printed with "Black Lives Matter" and images and phrases supporting the Dallas police victims and the African-American men who had died.

For John Carlos, mixing sports with activism has become "less of a choice for athletes and more of a responsibility. I think they now believe that they need to be a voice for the voiceless—especially people of color." In addition, Carlos expressed support for NFL quarterback Colin Kaepernick and other athletes who protested racial injustice by refusing to stand for the national anthem. Carlos linked it to the 1960s civil rights movement. "We were gardeners and caretakers. We till the earth. We plant the seeds. We water the ground. And what you see today is the fruit of our labor," Carlos said. "This is a movement, this is not a moment."

National Football League players Eric Reid (from left), Colin Kaepernick, and Eli Harold knelt during the national anthem in 2016.

were there. Being black, struggling with what we were going through, and they were trying to make a statement that still hasn't been heard."

But the white president of San Jose State University, Robert Clark, stood by his athletes. He called them "honorable young men dedicated to the cause of justice for the black people in our society." Many more in the San Jose State community and at other universities considered Smith and Carlos heroes. Carlos remembered admirers of the protest photograph telling him, "This picture here pushed a lot of us through school. We went to law school on the weight of what you've done." Carlos takes pride in knowing that "so many people find inspiration in that portrait. That's what I was born for."

As activists, Smith and Carlos hoped African-Americans were inspired by their actions. Harry Edwards explained that "the roots" of the protest "spring from the same seed that produced the sit-ins, the freedom rides and the rebellions in Watts, Detroit and Newark." While still in Mexico City, Carlos said, "We wanted all the black people in the world—the little grocer, the man with the shoe repair store—to know that when that medal hangs on my chest or Tommie's, it hangs on his also."

Dominis' photo is often called a black power salute, though Carlos and Smith never called it that. Smith called it a "human rights salute." Carlos explained that the protest was "a public statement

about what was happening, not just here in the United States for blacks, people of color, but people from all ethnic groups around this globe that were going through many [different] oppressions. Every ethnic group we were talking about was right there under the Olympic rings." Margaret Lambert, a champion German high jumper, had been barred from taking part in the 1936 Olympics by Hitler's government because she was Jewish. "When I saw those two guys with their fists up on the victory stand, it made my heart jump. It was beautiful," she said.

It took years for Smith and Carlos to earn
widespread admiration among Americans. Carlos
found strength from photographs like Dominis'.
"The image is still there," he said. "And the Olympics
are part of my history. I'm not going to run away
from that." Carlos eventually made peace with the
organization that rejected him, and he returned to
work for the U.S. Olympic Committee in preparation
for the 1984 Games in Los Angeles. Several years
later Smith told his story in a *Sports Illustrated*
article titled "A Courageous Stand."

Tommie Smith and the famous photo

Carlos and Smith were honored with a standing ovation in 2008 when they went on stage to receive the Arthur Ashe Courage Award. Winners of the award "reflect the spirit of Arthur Ashe, possessing strength in the face of adversity, courage in the face of peril and the willingness to stand up for their beliefs no matter what the cost." A month before the victory stand protest in 1968, Ashe had won the U.S. Open to become the first African-American man to win a major tennis title. Ashe shared OPHR's concerns about South Africa's racist society. He made a controversial trip to Johannesburg to play in a tournament to inspire black South Africans living without basic rights.

Dominis' photograph has not changed, but opinions about its subjects have. Once seen by some as a portrait of unpatriotic rebels, today many would agree with Olympic historian John MacAloon, who said the photo shows "an act of inspiration, passion and originality." Now Carlos and Smith are "heroes of the civil rights movement rather than villains of the black power phase," said sociologist Douglas Hartmann.

Visitors to the San Jose State campus today notice the pride the school takes in its piece of history. On a lawn near the Dr. Martin Luther King Jr. Library sits a 23-foot (7-m) -tall sculpture of Smith and Carlos on the victory stand. The sculpture was the idea of

students who had been inspired by Smith and Carlos' example of activism more than three decades earlier. In 2002 they urged the university to honor the men. Three years later, Tommie Smith, John Carlos, Peter Norman, and Harry Edwards attended the statue's unveiling on the 37th anniversary of the protest. A plaque reads, "Tommie Smith and John Carlos stood for justice, dignity, equality and peace." The statue is also near Robert D. Clark Hall, which was named for the university president who supported them in 1968.

John Carlos (left) and Tommie Smith were finally invited to the White House in 2016. They stood as they were honored by President Barack Obama. The relatives of Jesse Owens and other Olympians who were snubbed in 1936 were also honored.

The silver medalist's step on the platform is empty, offering an invitation for passersby to stand in Peter Norman's place, alongside Smith and Carlos. They might feel inspired to "take a stand," as the inscription on Norman's step urges. Captured on Dominis' film and now also depicted in steel and fiberglass, the protest continues to "ripple throughout the world," just as Martin Luther King Jr. said it could.

Timeline

June 6, 1944

Tommie Smith is born in Clarksville, Texas

June 5, 1945

John Carlos is born in Harlem, New York City

May 1954

In *Brown v. Board of Education*, the Supreme Court rules that separate is not equal and that segregation in public schools is unconstitutional

1967

The Olympic Project for Human Rights is formed

April 4, 1968

Martin Luther King Jr. is assassinated in Memphis, Tennessee; riots erupt in many U.S. cities

1964

President Lyndon Johnson signs the Civil Rights Act of 1964, which outlaws segregation

1965

Johnson pushes the Voting Rights Act through Congress, allowing millions of African-Americans to vote for the first time

October 17, 1968

Smith wins gold, Peter Norman wins silver, and Carlos wins bronze in the 200-meter sprint at the Mexico City Olympics; Smith and Carlos raise black-gloved fists during the national anthem

1969

Smith graduates from San Jose State and plays professional football for three years; he later earns a master's degree; Carlos helps lead San Jose State to its first national championship with wins in two sprints and a relay

1970

Carlos graduates from San Jose State and plays professional football for a short time

Timeline

1978

Smith is inducted into the National Track and Field Hall of Fame

1972

Smith becomes track coach at Oberlin College and teaches in the sociology department; he then spends 27 years as coach and professor at Santa Monica College until retiring in 2005

1984

Carlos works with the U.S. Olympic Committee in Los Angeles

2005

Smith and Carlos receive honorary doctorates from San Jose State University; they attend the dedication of a campus statue honoring their Olympic salute

2006

Peter Norman dies in Melbourne, Australia; Smith and Carlos serve as pallbearers

1985

Carlos becomes a track and field coach and guidance counselor at Palm Springs High School in California, where he works until retirement

2003

Carlos is inducted into the National Track and Field Hall of Fame

2008

Smith and Carlos are awarded the Arthur Ashe Award for Courage

2016

Smith and Carlos are named Olympic ambassadors; President Barack Obama honors them at the White House

Glossary

activist—person who works for social or political change

apartheid—former policy of racial segregation and discrimination in South Africa

boycott—to refuse as a group to take part in something as a protest

civil rights—rights that all Americans have to freedom and equal treatment under the law

discrimination—unfair treatment of people, often because of race, religion, gender, sexual preference, or age

integration—practice of allowing people of all races to attend public schools and enter other public places

massacre—needless killing of a group of helpless people

propaganda—information spread to try to influence the thinking of people; often not completely true or fair

segregation—practice of separating people of different races, income classes, or ethnic groups

sharecropper—farmer who works land owned by someone else in exchange for housing and part of the profits

unconstitutional—law or action that conflicts with the Constitution, the document that set up the government of the United States

Additional Resources

Further Reading

Herman, Gail. *What Are the Summer Olympics?* New York: Grosset & Dunlap, 2016.

Nardo, Don. *Massacre in Munich: How Terrorists Changed the Olympics and the World.* North Mankato, Minn.: Compass Point Books, 2016.

Tarrant-Reid, Linda. *Discovering Black America: From the Age of Exploration to the Twenty-First Century.* New York: Abrams Books for Young Readers, 2012.

Internet Sites

Use FactHound to find Internet sites related to this book. All of the sites on FactHound have been researched by our staff.

Here's all you do:
Visit *www.facthound.com*
Type in this code: 9780756555269

Critical Thinking Using the Common Core

How did the reaction of athletes to Jesse Owens' visit during the 1968 Olympics demonstrate the difference in attitude of activists in the 1960s and that of a generation earlier? (Key Ideas and Details)

Why was the San Jose State community an ideal place for activism to arise in the late 1960s? Consider specific people who were responsible. Also consider what conditions motivated them to organize. (Integration of Knowledge and Ideas)

Why do you think John Dominis' photo was once considered a portrait of unpatriotic Americans and decades later is considered a portrait of heroes? (Integration of Knowledge and Ideas)

Source Notes

Page 4, line 8: *Black Power Salute.* Documentary film by Geoff Small. BBC Four. 9 July 2008. 13 Oct. 2016. https://www.youtube.com/watch?v=jnvCiKUILAw

Page 4, line 18: Ibid.

Page 6, line 3: Juliet Spies-Gans. "47 Years Ago, Olympian John Carlos Raised His Fist for Equality." *The Huffington Post.* 16 Oct. 2015. 13 Oct. 2016. http://www.huffingtonpost.com/entry/john-carlos-47-years-olympics-salute_us_562157efe4b02f6a900c4fa2

Page 6, line 15: Simon Burnton. "50 stunning Olympic moments No. 13: Tommie Smith and John Carlos salute." *The Guardian.* 8 Feb. 2012. 13 Oct. 2016. https://www.theguardian.com/sport/blog/2012/feb/08/olympic-moments-tommie-smith-john-carlos

Page 6, line 21: *Black Power Salute.*

Page 6, line 29: David Davis. "Olympic Athletes Who Took a Stand." *Smithsonian Magazine.* August 2008. 13 Oct. 2016. http://www.smithsonianmag.com/people-places/olympic-athletes-who-took-a-stand-593920/?no-ist

Page 7, line 4: Ben Cosgrove. "The Black Power Salute That Rocked the 1968 Olympics." *Time.* 27 Sept. 2014. 13 Oct. 2016. http://time.com/3880999/black-power-salute-tommie-smith-and-john-carlos-at-the-1968-olympics/

Page 9, col. 1, line 4: Ben Cosgrove. "Photographer Spotlight: John Dominis." *Time.* 20 Dec. 2013. 13 Oct. 2016. http://time.com/3524708/photographer-spotlight-john-dominis/

Page 10, line 12: *Black Power Salute.*

Page 10, line 20: "A Stubborn Protest Jars the Games: Amid Gold Medals, Raised Black Fists." *Life.* 1 Nov. 1968, p. 64C.

Page 10, line 25: "John Carlos, 1968 Olympic U.S. Medalist, on the Revolutionary Sports Moment that Changed the World." Democracy Now! 12 Oct. 2011. 13 Oct. 2016. http://www.democracynow.org/2011/10/12/john_carlos_1968_olympic_us_medalist

Page 12, line 7: Joyful Gypsy. "Tlatelolco Massacre (Mexico City)." CNN iReport. 2 Oct. 2009. 13 Oct. 2016. http://ireport.cnn.com/docs/DOC-336863

Page 16, line 21: Martin Luther King Jr. "Letter from a Birmingham Jail. 16 April 1963." African Studies Center—University of Pennsylvania. 13 Oct. 2016. https://www.africa.upenn.edu/Articles_Gen/Letter_Birmingham.html

Page 19, line 3: Martin Luther King Jr. "I Have a Dream …" National Archives. 13 Oct. 2016. https://www.archives.gov/press/exhibits/dream-speech.pdf

Page 20, line 20: Michael T. Kaufman. "Stokely Carmichael, Rights Leader Who Coined 'Black Power,' Dies at 57." *The New York Times.* 16 Nov. 1998. 13 Oct. 2016. http://www.nytimes.com/1998/11/16/us/stokely-carmichael-rights-leader-who-coined-black-power-dies-at-57.html

Page 20, line 29: "Malcolm X. Make It Plain." American Experience. PBS. 19 May 2005. 13 Oct. 2016. http://www.pbs.org/wgbh/amex/malcolmx/peopleevents/e_civilrights.html

Page 21, line 3: Malcolm X. "Message to the Grass Roots. 10 Nov. 1963." History of the Civil Rights Movement. 13 Oct. 2016. http://xroads.virginia.edu/~public/civilrights/a0147.html

Page 21, line 7: "I Have a Dream …"

Page 22, line 6: "Malcolm X's Speech at the Founding Rally of the Organization of Afro-American Unity 1964." Black Past. 13 Oct. 2016. http://www.blackpast.org/1964-malcolm-x-s-speech-founding-rally-organization-afro-american-unity

Page 23, col. 1, line 12: "The Ten-Point Program." Marxist History Archive. 15 Oct. 1966. 13 Oct. 2016. https://www.marxists.org/history/usa/workers/black-panthers/1966/10/15.htm

Page 23, col. 2, line 3: Robert Lipsyte. "Clay Refuses Army Oath; Stripped of Boxing Crown." *The New York Times.* 29 April 1967. 13 Oct. 2016. https://www.nytimes.com/books/98/10/25/specials/ali-army.html

Page 24, line 4: "Stokely Carmichael, Rights Leader Who Coined 'Black Power,' Dies at 57."

Page 24, line 11: Ibid.

Page 26, line 8: Vernon M. Briggs Jr. "Report of the National Advisory Commission on Civil Disorders: A Review Article." *Journal of Economic Issues,* June 1968. 13 Oct. 2016. Cornell University IRL School. http://digitalcommons.ilr.cornell.edu/cgi/viewcontent.cgi?article=1047&context=hrpubs

Page 26, line 15: "The Assassination of Martin Luther King Jr., 1968." LBJ. The Presidents. American Experience. PBS. 13 Oct. 2016. http://www.pbs.org/wgbh/americanexperience/features/primary-resources/lbj-assassination/

Page 27, line 1: "Hoover and the FBI." PBS. 13 Oct. 2016. http://www.pbs.org/hueypnewton/people/people_hoover.html

Page 27, line 9: "Malcolm X. Make It Plain."

Page 28, line 3: Joseph M. Sheehan. "2 Black Power Advocates Ousted From Olympics." *The New York Times.* 19 Oct. 1968, pp. 1 and 45.

Page 28, line 6: Paul Vitello. "John Dominis, a Star Photographer for Life Magazine, Dies at 92." *The New York Times.* 31 Dec. 2013. 13 Oct. 2016. http://www.nytimes.com/2014/01/01/arts/design/john-dominis-a-star-life-magazine-photographer-dies.html?_r=0

Page 28, line 13: "1968: Black athletes make silent protest." BBC. 13 Oct. 2016. http://news.bbc.co.uk/onthisday/hi/dates/stories/october/17/newsid_3535000/3535348.stm

Page 28, line 23: Ibid

Page 29, line 1: Jason Lewis. "Black History: Political and social statements at the Olympics." *Los Angeles Sentinel.* 18 Feb. 2011. 13 Oct. 2016. https://lasentinel.net/black-history-political-and-social-statements-at-the-olympics.html

Page 29, line 4: Dave Zirin. "The explosive 1968 Olympics." *International Socialist Review.* September-October 2008. 13 Oct. 2016. http://www.isreview.org/issues/61/feat-zirin.shtml

Page 30, line 4: Caroline Frost. "John Carlos Remembers His Scandalous Podium Salute At The Mexico Olympics 1968." *The Huffington Post.* 22 May 2012. 13 Oct. 2016. http://www.huffingtonpost.co.uk/2013/10/17/john-carlos-mexico-olympics-podium-salute_n_1536484.html

Page 32, line 2: Robert Lipsyte. "Backtalk: Silent Salute, Ringing Impact." *The New York Times.* 17 Oct. 1993. 13 Oct. 2016. http://www.nytimes.com/1993/10/17/sports/backtalk-silent-salute-ringing-impact.html?pagewanted=all

Page 32, line 10: "The explosive 1968 Olympics."

Page 32, line 19: "1968: Black athletes make silent protest."

Page 33, line 1: Sandy Banks. "Trailblazing athletes seek to ease path for next generation." *Los Angeles Times.* 13 Oct. 2014. 13 Oct. 2016. http://www.latimes.com/local/la-me-1014-banks-olympic-protest-20141014-column.html

Page 33, line 6: "The explosive 1968 Olympics."

Page 33, line 13: *Black Power Salute.*

Page 34, line 24: "Tommie Smith." NBC News. 11 Feb. 2008. 13 Oct. 2016. https://archives.nbclearn.com/portal/site/k-12/flatview?cuecard=5742

Page 34, line 27: "The explosive 1968 Olympics."

Page 35, line 6: *Black Power Salute.*

Page 35, line 10: "The explosive 1968 Olympics."

Page 36, line 6: Ibid.

Page 37, line 6: Ibid.

Page 37, line 17: Dave Zirin. "Fists of Freedom: An Olympic Story Not Taught in School."Zinn Education Project. PBS. 13 Oct. 2016. http://www.pbs.org/newshour/extra/wp-content/uploads/sites/2/2014/02/All-docs-for-Human-Rights-lesson-2.pdf

Page 38, line 3: *Black Power Salute.*

Page 38, line 7: Ibid.

Page 38, line 15: "The explosive 1968 Olympics."

Page 38, line 19: *Black Power Salute.*

Page 38, line 24: "The explosive 1968 Olympics."

Page 39, col. 1, line 2: "AOC denies blacklisting Norman over Olympic protest." Australian Broadcasting Corporation. 20 Aug. 2012. 13 Oct. 2016. http://www.abc.net.au/news/2012-08- 21/aoc-denies-blacklisting-norman- over-olympic- protest/4211788

Page 39, col. 1, line 7: James Montague. "The third man: The forgotten Black Power hero." CNN. 25 April 2012. 13 Oct. 2016. http://edition.cnn.com/2012/04/24/sport/olympics-norman-black-power/

Page 39, col. 1, line 13: Ibid.

Page 39, col. 2, line 4: Ibid

Page 39, col. 2, line 7: "50 stunning Olympic moments No. 13: Tommie Smith and John Carlos salute."

Page 39, col. 2, line 10: Hilary Whiteman. "Apology urged for Australian Olympian in 1968 black power protest." CNN. 21 Aug. 2012. 13 Oct. 2016. http://www.cnn.com/2012/08/21/world/asia/australia-norman-olympic-apology/

Page 40, line 4: "John Dominis, a Star Photographer for Life Magazine, Dies at 92."

Page 40, line 23: Gary Younge. "The man who raised a black power salute at the 1968 Olympic Games." *The Guardian.* 30 March 2012. 13 Oct. 2016. https://www.theguardian.com/world/2012/mar/30/black-power-salute-1968-olympics

Page 41, line 2: Ibid.

Page 42, line 3: "47 Years Ago, Olympian John Carlos Raised His Fist for Equality."

Page 42, line 9: "The Black Power Salute That Rocked the 1968 Olympics."

Page 42, line 13: Allen Barra. "Fists Raised, but Not in Anger." *The New York Times.* 22 Aug. 2008. 13 Oct. 2016. http://www.nytimes.com/2008/08/23/opinion/23barra.html?_r=0

Page 43, line 5: Remarks by the President Welcoming the 2016 USA Olympic and Paralympic Teams. Office of the Press Secretary. The White House. 29 Sept. 2016. 13 Oct. 2016. https://www.whitehouse.gov/the-press-office/2016/09/29/remarks-president-welcoming-2016-usa-olympic-and-paralympic-teams

Page 43, line 20: Dave Zirin. "Forty-Five Years Later, John Carlos and Tommie Smith Have Never Been More Relevant." *The Nation.* 16 Oct. 2013. 13 Oct. 2016. http://www.thenation.com/article/forty-five-years-later-john-carlos-and-tommie-smith-have-never-been-more-relevant/

Page 43, line 27: Phaedra Trethan. "'68 Olympian John Carlos talks race, sports at Rutgers-Camden." *Courier-Post.* 30 March 2016. 13 Oct. 2016. http://www.courierpostonline.com/story/news/2016/03/30/68-olympian-john-carlos-talks-race-sports-rutgers-camden/82440598/

Page 44, line 7: Sally Jenkins. "At Sochi Olympics, the podium can be a platform." *The Washington Post.* 23 Aug. 2013. 14 Oct. 2016. https://www.washingtonpost.com/sports/olympics/at-sochi-olympics-the-podium-can-be-a-platform/2013/08/23/943f58b6-0c04-11e3-b87c-476db8ac34cd_story.html

Page 44, line 11: "The explosive 1968 Olympics."

Page 44, line 23: *Black Power Salute.*

Page 45, line 1: "2 Black Power Advocates Ousted From Olympics."

Page 46, line 1: *Black Power Salute.*

Page 46, line 7: "The explosive 1968 Olympics."

Page 46, line 15: Todd Boyd. *African Americans and Popular Culture.* Vol. 1. Westport, Conn.: Praeger Publishers, 2008, p. 187.

Page 46, line 28: *Black Power Salute.*

Page 47, line 2: Ibid.

Page 48, line 2: *African Americans and Popular Culture*, p. 187.

Page 48, line 5: "Backtalk: Silent Salute, Ringing Impact."

Page 48, line 13: Foster, Richard J. *Mark Spitz: The Extraordinary Life of an Olympic Champion.* Santa Monica, Calif.: Santa Monica Press, 2008, p. 74.

Page 48, line 19: "Forty-Five Years Later, John Carlos and Tommie Smith Have Never Been More Relevant."

Page 48, line 22: Ibid.

Page 48, line 25: "Backtalk: Silent Salute, Ringing Impact."

Page 49, col. 1, line 21: "LeBron James on social activism: 'We all have to do better.'" ESPN. 14 July 2016. 13 Oct. 2016. http://www.espn.com/espys/2016/story/_/id/17060953/espys-carmelo-anthony-chris-paul-dwyane-wade-lebron-james-call-athletes-promote-change

Page 49, col. 1, line 28: Ibid.

Page 49, col. 2, line 5: Jack Buehrer. "Olympics Black Power Heroes Are Still Waiting for an Apology." *The Daily Beast.* 4 Aug. 2016. 13 Oct. 2016. http://www.thedailybeast.com/articles/2016/08/04/olympics-black-power-heroes-are-still-waiting-for-an-apology.html

Page 49, col. 2, line 11: Curtis Skinner. "Olympian known for raised fist calls NFL protests 'shock treatment.'" Reuters. 12 Sept. 2016. 13 Oct. 2016. http://www.reuters.com/article/us-nfl-anthem-johncarlos-idUSKCN11I2PR

Page 50, line 6: "50 stunning Olympic moments No. 13: Tommie Smith and John Carlos salute."

Page 50, line 11: "Trailblazing athletes seek to ease path for next generation."

Page 50, line 14: "The man who raised a black power salute at the 1968 Olympic Games."

Page 50, line 18: Douglas Hartman. *Race, Culture, and the Revolt of the Black Athlete: The 1968 Olympic Protests And Their Aftermath.* Chicago: The University of Chicago Press, 2003, p. 41.

Page 50, line 22: "A Stubborn Protest Jars the Games: Amid Gold Medals, Raised Black Fists."

Page 50, line 28: "Tommie Smith: Why I Gave Black Power Salute." Sky News. 11 July 2012. 13 Oct. 2016. http://news.sky.com/story/tommie-smith-why-i-gave-black-power-salute-10476202

Page 50, line 29: "47 Years Ago, Olympian John Carlos Raised His Fist for Equality."

Page 51, line 9: "The man who raised a black power salute at the 1968 Olympic Games."

Page 52, line 4: Ibid.

Page 53, line 4: Arthur Ashe Award. ESPN. 14 Oct. 2016. http://espn.go.com/espys/arthurasheaward

Page 53, line 19: *Race, Culture, and the Revolt of the Black Athlete: The 1968 Olympic Protests And Their Aftermath*, p. 20.

Page 53, line 21: *Black Power Salute.*

Page 54, line 7: "50 stunning Olympic moments No. 13: Tommie Smith and John Carlos salute."

Page 55, line 8: "At Sochi Olympics, the podium can be a platform."

Select Bibliography

Axthelm, Pete. "Boos and a beating for Tommie." *Sports Illustrated*. 29 Jan. 1968. 14 Oct. 2016. http://www.si.com/vault/1968/01/29/670170/boos-and-a-beating-for-tommie?

Black Past.org: Remembered & Reclaimed. blackpast.org

Black Power Salute. BBC documentary directed by Geoff Small; produced by Natasha Dack, 2008.

Briggs, Vernon M., Jr. "Report of the National Advisory Commission on Civil Disorders: A Review Article." *Journal of Economic Issues*, June 1968. 13 Oct. 2016. Cornell University IRL School. http://digitalcommons.ilr.cornell.edu/cgi/viewcontent.cgi?article=1047&context=hrpubs

Boyd, Todd. *African Americans and Popular Culture*. Vol. 1. Westport, Conn.: Praeger Publishers, 2008.

Burnton, Simon. "50 stunning Olympic moments No. 13: Tommie Smith and John Carlos salute." *The Guardian*. 8 Feb. 2012. 13 Oct. 2016. https://www.theguardian.com/sport/blog/2012/feb/08/olympic-moments-tommie-smith-john-carlos

Cosgrove, Ben. "Photographer Spotlight: John Dominis." *Time*. 20 Dec. 2013. 13 Oct. 2016. http://time.com/3524708/photographer-spotlight-john-dominis/

Davis, David. "Olympic Athletes Who Took a Stand." *Smithsonian Magazine*. August 2008. 13 Oct. 2016. http://www.smithsonianmag.com/people-places/olympic-athletes-who-took-a-stand-593920/?no-ist

Hartmann, Douglas. *Race, Culture, and the Revolt of the Black Athlete: The 1968 Olympic Protests And Their Aftermath*. Chicago: The University of Chicago Press, 2003.

Korpe, Prerana. "The Birth Of *Life*, 79 Years Ago." Newseum. 23 Nov. 2015. 14 Oct. 2016. http://www.newseum.org/2015/11/23/the-birth-of-life-79-years-ago-today/

Montague, James. "The third man: The forgotten Black Power hero." CNN. 25 April 2012. 13 Oct. 2016. http://edition.cnn.com/2012/04/24/sport/olympics-norman-black-power/

Moore, Kenny. "A Courageous Stand." *Sports Illustrated*. 5 Aug. 1991. 14 Oct. 2016. http://www.si.com/vault/1991/08/05/124647/the-1968-olympics-a-courageous-stand-first-of-a-two-part-series-in-68-olympians-tommie-smith-and-john-carlos-raised-their-fists-for-racial-justice

Murphy, Austin. "John Carlos." *Sports Illustrated*. 14 July 2008. 14 Oct. 2016. http://www.si.com/vault/1969/12/31/105711810/john-carlos

Smith, Maureen Margaret. "Frozen Fists in Speed City: The Statue as Twenty-First-Century Reparations." *Journal of Sport History*. Fall 2009, p. 393. 13 Oct. 2016. http://library.la84.org/SportsLibrary/JSH/JSH2009/JSH3603/jsh3603j.pdf

Stayner, Guy. "Australian in famous Olympics protest to get apology." Australian Broadcasting Corporation. 20 Aug. 2012. 14 Oct. 2016. http://www.abc.net.au/7.30/content/2012/s3571974.htm

"A Stubborn Protest Jars the Games: Amid Gold Medals, Raised Black Fists." *Life*. 1 Nov. 1968, p. 264C.

Zirin, Dave. "Fists of Freedom: An Olympic Story Not Taught in School."Zinn Education Project. PBS. 13 Oct. 2016. http://www.pbs.org/newshour/extra/wp-content/uploads/sites/2/2014/02/All-docs-for-Human-Rights-lesson-2.pdf

Index

About the Author

As a former teacher, Danielle Smith-Llera taught children to think and write about literature before writing books for them herself. As the spouse of a diplomat, she enjoys living in both Washington, D.C., and overseas in countries such as India, Jamaica, and Romania.